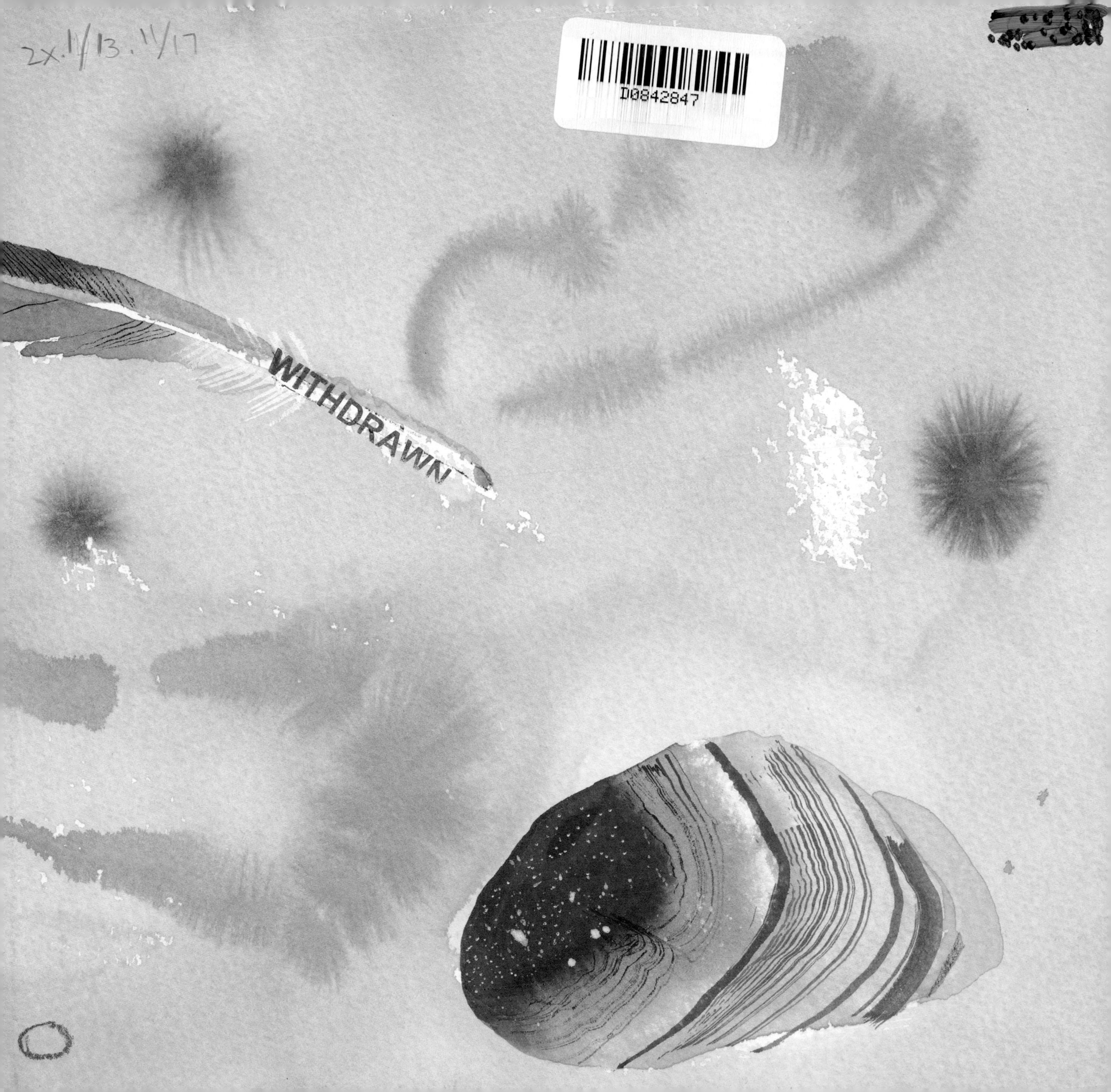

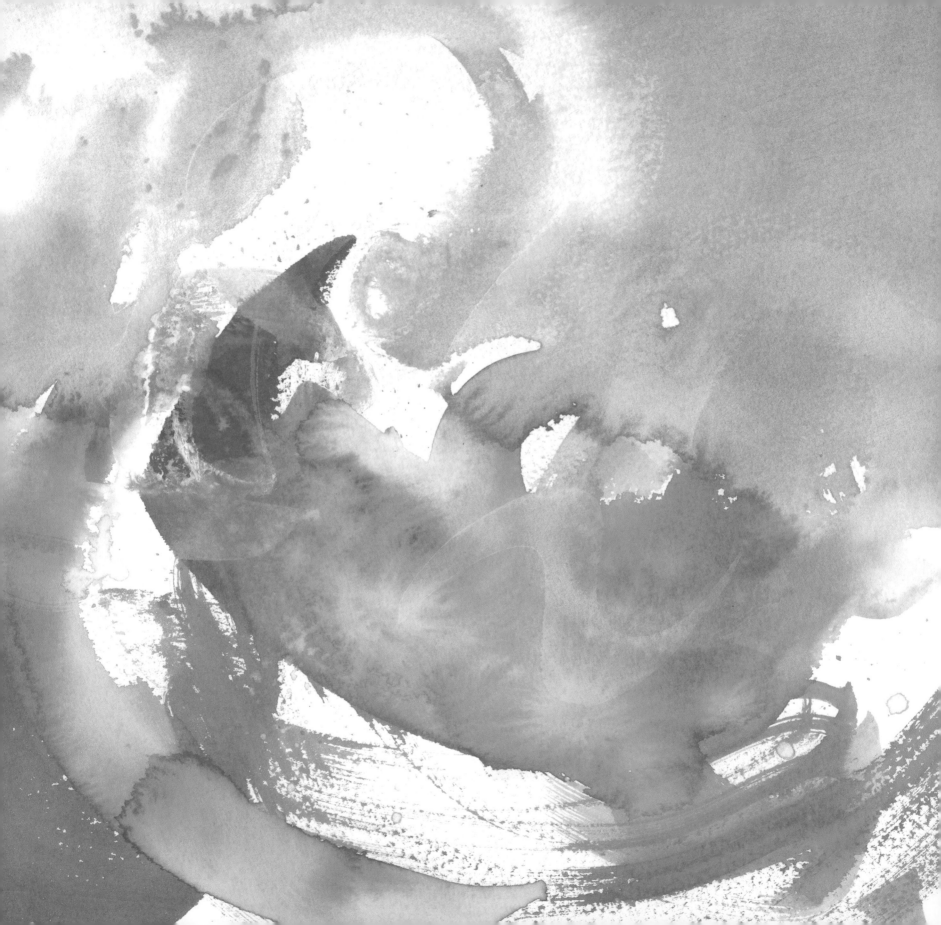

Water Sings Blue

Ocean Poems

by Kate Coombs *illustrated by* Meilo So

chronicle books · san francisco

Song of the Boat

Push away from the stillness of the nut-brown land,
from the road that leads to the shore.

Push away from the town with its tight tree roots,
from its closed brown shutters and doors.

Push away—heave-ho—from the heavy brown pier,
from its pilings huddled and dull.

For the water sings blue and the sky does, too,
and the sea lets you fly like a gull.

Seagulls

Seagulls remind me of beagles—
all that they think of is food.
Yet seagulls can soar through the sky
the minute they get in the mood.
And when seagulls take wing,
they become a new thing,
attaining some dignity.
But beagles are round
and remain on the ground,
pretty much dignity-free.

Sand's Story

We used to be rocks,
we used to be stones.
We stood proud as castles,
altars, and thrones.

Once we were massive,
looming in rings,
holding up temples
and posing as kings.

Now we grind and we grumble,
humbled and grave,
at the touch of our breaker
and maker, the wave.

Tide Pool Shopping

I'm going shopping at the tide pool.
They carry everything there—
mussels by the bushel
and three kinds of barnacle,
starfish and gobies to spare.

My mama gave me a shopping list.
I know I can find what she likes—
blennies for pennies,
beadlet anemones,
and urchins with lavender spikes.

I'll bring it all home in a basket.
Then mama can fix us a feast—
prawns by the dozens
and octopus cousins,
plus some kind of lobstery beast.

Today I'm shopping at the tide pool.
Maybe I'll see you there, too,
with your kittiwake pals
and the oystercatcher gals—
I'll save some limpets for you!

Sea Urchin

The sea urchin fell in love with a fork.
With a tremble of purple spines,
    she told her mother, "He's tall, not a ball,
        but just look at his wonderful tines!"

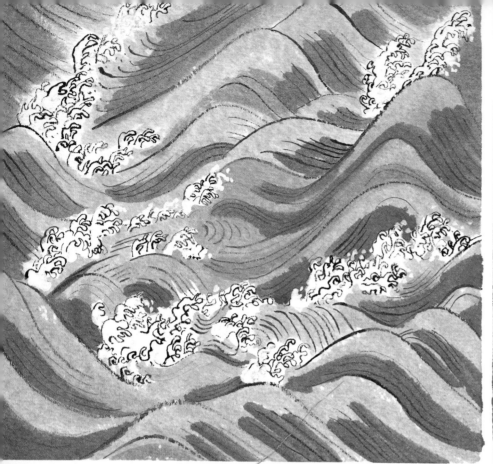

Shimmer and run, catch the sun.
Ripple thin, catch the wind.

Shift and splash, drift and dash.
Slow and gray, foggy day.

Whisper hush, murmur shush.
Swell and sigh, otter lullaby.

Journey on with a yawn.
Swirl and swish, play with fish.

Roll green, rise and lean—
wake and roar and strike the shore!

What the Waves Say

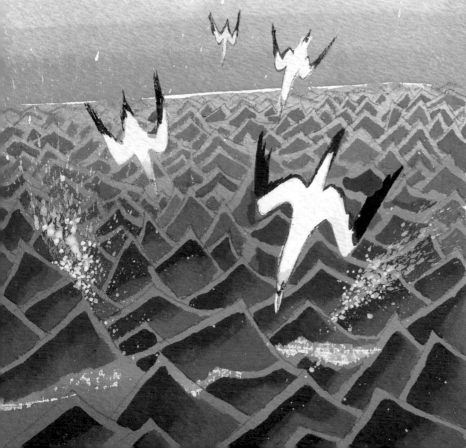

Prayer of the Little Fish

Keep my gills and keep my fins,
keep me safe in the cool dark,
keep me from the hungry eyes
of the swift and toothful shark.

Find me tender plankton sweet,
help me swim with grace and care,
and please, O Lord, protect me from
the high, dry, breathless air.

Water Artist

I stroke water over water
with my fantail brush.

I use my fins to stipple.
I'm in no rush.

Small currents ripple
exactly as I planned.

I'm a water artist.
You wouldn't understand.

Jellyfish Kitchen

The prim bell jar
with ruffled rim
my grandma used
to cover cake
has learned to swim.

Where bundts once lay
in sturdy rings,
this dome conceals
a frosted sting.

Not Really Jelly

You're not really jelly,
you're not really fish—
you're free-floating noodles
escaped from a dish,
all slither and jiggle
and tremble and squish.

Jellyfish

Deep water shimmers.
  A wind-shape passes,
kimono trailing.

Blue Whale

Rolling your belly like a tide,
sweeping the little fish aside,
billow and swell of midnight blue,
you're as grand as a planet
passing through.

Shipwreck

Here lie the bones
of twenty trees,
lost far from home
under gallons of seas.

Oarfish

Dragon doesn't hide her magic
in a crooked mountain cave.
She dwells down deep and deeper
where the sea feels like a grave.

If a lantern fish is near her
and can shed a little light,
you'll glimpse the mythic creature
flowing by you in the night,

with her silver undulation,
fifty feet from tail to head,
with her glorious and rippling
crest of incantation red.

Gulper Eel

Black holes usually spin through space,
lurking by planets and stars,
but there's one in the gulper's gullet,
stuck like a dollop of tar.
He opens and opens and opens
and opens and opens his jaw—
till the proudest fish has vanished
in that astronomical maw.

Sea Turtle

There's a wide green map
on sea turtle's back.
Currents? She knows
their flows, never slows,
needn't stop for directions
wherever she goes,
flapping her elegant
paddle-shaped toes.

Octopus Ink

The famous author hesitates
to pick his pen up.
He is shy. But wait!
He autographs the water
with a single word—
good-bye.

We are busy.
We are growing.
We don't care where
you are going.

We are cousins.
We're a throng.
We are wide
and we are strong.

We are reaching,
stretching high.
Pretty soon
we'll own the sky.

We are golden.
We are pretty.
We are coral.
We are city.

Coral

Shark

He circles and stares
with a broken-glass grin,
his body's a dagger,
he has lion's-tongue skin.

He slides through the water
like a rumor, like a sneer.
He's a quick twist of hunger.
He's the color of fear.

Nudibranch

The nudibranch
has dropped his clothes
in a spot not even
his slug mother knows.

Ocean Realty

My name's Frank Hermit.
Here—take my card.
So you want a house
with a porch and yard?

I have listings for periwinkles,
whelks, and wentletraps;
turbans, tops, and moon shells;
a palatial conch, perhaps?

That one's not available—
I'm waiting for the snail
to vacate his townhouse
and put it up for sale.

But this place has a deck
and a nice view of the land—
beachfront property
is always in demand!

Old Driftwood
has been to sea
and come back home
unexpectedly.

Gnarled sailor,
now he sits high
up on the beach
beyond the tide,

telling of mermaids
and whales thi-i-i-s big
to all the attentive
astonished twigs.

*Old
Driftwood*

Tideline

Ocean draws on the sand
with trinkets of shell and stone,
the way I write on the sidewalk
with a stick of chalk at home.

She signs her name in letters
long and wavy and clear,
saying "Don't forget me—

I was here,
          wasss h e r e
               wasssss h e r e . . ."

A seashell for my sister Karen —K. C.

To my old man —M. S.

Text © 2012 by Kate Coombs.
Illustrations © 2012 by Meilo So.
All rights reserved. No part of this book may be reproduced in
any form without written permission from the publisher.

Library of Congress Cataloging-in-Publication Data
Coombs, Kate.
Water sings blue : ocean poems / by Kate Coombs;
illustrated by Meilo So.
p. cm.
ISBN 978-0-8118-7284-3 (alk. paper)
1. Sea poetry. I. So, Meilo. II. Title.
PS3603.O5796W38 2012
811'.6—dc22
2010030163

Typeset in Cochin.
The illustrations in this book were rendered in watercolor.

Manufactured in China.

10 9 8 7 6 5 4 3 2

Chronicle Books LLC
680 Second Street, San Francisco, California 94107

www.chroniclekids.com